Ibn Khalikan

Contents

Introduction

Afterword

Contents:

Introduction:

The purpose of this little book is to explore the contribution made by the Kurdish people in the fields of Science, philosophy, literature, and art throughout the history of Islam, to promote peace and social harmony in the Middle East, particularly within the era of the Ayiubid Empire.

The Ayiubid Empire united the ethnic, racial, and religious divisions [of the area stretching from modern day (insert country/region) to modern day (insert country/region)] to protect the people from occupation, enslavement, plunder and subjugation in the name of religious, ethnic, and racial rivalries. This shows how art, science and a peaceful social harmony flourished.

This book consists of extracts from the life of a few known Kurdish leaders, scientists, philosophers, poets and scholars. Influential figures from other ethnic groups have been chosen either for their close ties, or direct involvement with the Kurdish establishment of the Ayiubid Empire. The purpose of this book is to show how art, science, and social harmony was achieved with the valour and virtues of the Kurdish leadership that is mellowed in a humane and true religious partnership to achieve peace and stability in the Middle East.

Ibn Khalikan's book was researched and published by the Irish scholar William McGauin Di Slaine, who regarded Ibn Khalikan's book as one of the first and finest historical books written in the history of Islam.

Ibn Khalika's book has been translated to English German, French, and numerous other languages. Historians and scholars have used this work to research and publish academic texts, books, and essays about the scholars, poets, and scientists in the history of Islam.

In this book, a number of known Kurdish known scholars and poets have been selected from the Works of Ibn Khalikan, *'Wafayiti Ayian wa Anbi Zaman'* *'the Arabic name of the book'*

The kind of social interactions is revealed through the use of poetry. It was one of the premier medias of the elite, and was used as the method of correspondence and communication. The tender, exotic, and beautiful language is used to conjure and describe, social interactions, the importance of family, highbred intellectual interactions, and the highly romantic spoken language that often used with a playful exaggeration to express people's devotedness and passion.

This is an exotic book, where poems narrate various aspects of social life with mesmerising colourful images of spiritual devotedness, poetic imagination, and lyrics with various tenets of spiritual, romance, and humane compassion.

Ibn Khalikan 1211 – 1282

Ibn Khalikan, was a Kurdish scholar, historian, a judge and a poet, born in Erbil on the 22nd September 1211. He spent eighteen years researching an compiling his book, *'Waffaiati Ayian wa Anbai Zaman'* a dictionary compiling the works of known scholars, philosophers, leaders and poets throughout the history of Islam. He studied in Erbil, Mosel, Damascus, and Cairo. He studied jurisprudence, law, Arabic grammar and philosophy.

In Egypt, he was the deputy of the Egypt's head judge. He returned to Damascus to become the head judge of Syria. He retired in 1281, and died on 30th October 1282. His book, *'Waffaiati Ayian wa Anbai Zaman'* consists of 2,700 pages, spread across four volumes. He was acknowledged for his essays and poetry during his lifetime, and after his death.

The following are a few of his poems:

For my Love

The image of your beauty has taken

All the boundaries of my mind.

Thinking of you so far away, but we are still
So close.

It was like a mythical romance that so often
You refused to confess.

You are one from my own folk, as

I am waiting for your homecoming.

So many, who are waiting in despair,

Would you clearly see their reason?

I swear with almighty God,

For the ones who are after you with passion.

They are like offenders who cover their sins
With your scarf.

So desperately are seeking forgiveness,

As, they are in fear of being exposed.

He is the one, who suffers from loneliness,

He is going grey with passing years and
Getting aged.

For my Love (a variation)

*Your image is set in the boundaries of my
Mind.*

*Thinking of you even when you are so far
Away*

*My heart has become your familiar abode.
When you are so far away, but I am*

*Preoccupied with your discourse, as we are
So intimately close*

*It is just like a mythical fairy tale so often you
Were anxious and hesitant.*

*As you are one of my folk, I'm looking
Forward for your coming back.*

*For some people who are inflicted with
Passion*

*But, with the rational sense, you can find a
Right path,*

*I am the only one who is truly fond of you.
Let us meet again and forget whatever has
Passed*

The ones who passionately sought your
Attention, I swear to God

They try to hide their sins with your scarf
When their faults are exposed

Now, he is the one, who suffers from
Loneliness, he is going grey.

With passing time, he is becoming so
Helpless and aged.

Ibn Asayiegh, a poet from Damascus wrote about Ibn Khalikan when he was returning to Damascus from Egypt

You are coming back:

Amongst all the City's inhabitants,

*There was no one who was not happy with your
Home coming.*

*Whatever happened so far, so now it is the time
Of reflection, at last, as there is happiness after
The long time of distress.*

*The joy you've brought us with inspiration it is the
Time of fortune and wisdom*

*After being away for so long, your return has
Brought the reign of joy, it was the era of unjust,*

*And whatever have passed it is the time of Re-
flection and we should reconcile and forget.*

Ibn Khalikan Died in Damascus, Syria after a
year retirement in October 1282.

*Extracts taken from the introduction to Ibn Khalikan's
work that consists of 2700 pages in four volumes.
'Wafayat al Ayian wa Anbai Zaman.'*

Murtada Sharazuri 1073 – 1117

Abdulla Qasim Muzafar Ali Qasim Sharazuri, was called Murtada, he was a Judge and a religious scholar. He was the son of Kamal al Din Sharazuri, the head judge of Damascus and advisor of the Zanjid ruler Nour al Din Mahmood Zanjid, the Turkish Zanjid King of Syria. He was born in Mosel in 1073. He worked as a Jurist, Essayist and a poet, he was known for writing religious Sonnets and known as a Sophist poet. He lived and studied in Baghdad for many years. He died in 1117, in Mosel and was buried at the cemetery of the Sharazuri family in Mosel.

The Following is an example of his sophist poems:

The Sparkling Flame

The sparkling flame of her fire is seen from
Far away at sunset.

Although the camel-man wanted to sing, but
Was not able to continue.

Our desert guide stopped, and didn't know
What to do, he was so perplexed,

I was engrossed looking at the flame, I was
Helpless, and my recollection was weak.

I knew I was so far away, far from my love
And I was in despair.

I was so involved, inflicted, and there was no
hope.

The heart that you have known so well, has
Been in pain from passion for so long,

I turned to my friends and said,

Is that Layla's fire, are you aware?'

When they turned to me and looked so hard
And were astonished,

*Could not look for long and turned away with
Disgust.*

They turned away, looked angry, and fed up.

*I was facing so many questions, like I was
Struck with a thunder bolt.*

*They wondered whether these illusions came
Through with a spiritual spell.*

*Nonetheless, I turned again and on my way,
As if my love was sitting at the back, I
Thought.*

*That was what the nature of romance Re-
quired me to do, and so the fire continued.*

*We were getting closer until we got to an
Abandoned, derelict wasteland.*

*Yet, we carried on, I took a deep breath, and
I was sad.*

*'Who were the ones, who used to live here?'
I just wondered.*

*When I asked with a shout, in reply there
Was a voice that said,*

*'There used to be an injured man, a captive
Of love who was alone, what brought you*

Here?'

I am a traveller, I need rest. That was my

*Reply; 'can you put me up for the night?
Can I be a guest?*

*Is there any food, where is the gesture of
Welcome?'*

*Then they showed me the middle of the
Wasteland,*

*'That is where you should stay and wait until
We kill your camel for lunch.*

*Whoever reaches here, there is no way to
Escape.'*

*'Should I give in my cart of travel?' I
Shouted:*

*'But now, I want to reach the fire where is the
Way?'*

*Here we stayed in this place, where some
Others had stayed in the past.*

*The ones, who used to taste the wine of
Love.*

*The passionate desire for love eliminated all
Aspects of happiness.*

*They became obvious scars of annihilation,
And didn't leave any traces of being.*

*Here is nothing, no trace, no complain, no
Tears.*

*As if there were only dreaming that had
Become like exhibition of their remains.*

*They lost wisdom, desperate; far away and
Forgotten.*

*Amongst those, someone was passionately
Trying to show the way.*

*'If one of those reached their aims, their
Fame would become like a sacred name.*

*With its enormous sanctity, as words of God
Will be important for everyone,' he said.*

Murtada Sharzuri died in Mosel in 1117, and buried in the Sharzuri famly cemetery in Mosel.

Ibn khalikan volume 2 page 29-32

'Qadi Fadil' 1135 – 1200 (The first minister
of Sultan Saladin.

Jamil Abd al Rahim leqmy, Ascallani, also
known as 'Qadi Fadil,' was born in the town
of Ascallon. He was part of the tribe of
Laqm, and became known as 'Qadi Fadil'
with the surname of Mujarid al Din, son of
Ashraff Beha al Din Majd Ali. He became the
first minister of Sultan Saladin. He swiftly became recognised for his remarkable creative
writing abilities, composing fiction, romantic
poetry, prose, and essays.

Ibn khalikan met a man who knew Qadi Fadil
and he told him, *'he [Qadi Fadil] had written
so much beautiful prose, essays, and poems, one could fill nearly fifty books of his
writing.'*

Emad al Din Esfahani, Sultan Saladin's advisor and minister, once wrote about Qadi al
Fadil: 'he *was the master of writing and
pens, with artistic expressions and elo-
quence, his ability in precision and beauty
was so high in Arabic Language, no one else
in the history of writing could be found to*

*equal his competence, or be able to go close
to his beautiful style of writing.'*

During Qadi Fadil's life, the mode of writing
was strict and written like religious doctrines;
he set himself apart with his unique and original style. Methods of creative writing were
like a science that had special rules and a
particular style, like arranging the decoration
of a boutique of flowers.

He managed his duty of correspondence for
the Ayiubid Empire, with wisdom, cleverness,
as if the form of his writing designed with
pearls, diamonds, and jewels engraved into
his style of writings. When he was in a right
mood, he would construct his essay in just
the space of an hour.

In the following poem he says:

A Castle

Oh, my mighty God,

A castle on a lonely height, like a hawk

Perched on the mountain cliff

It was like a lonely star in the sky, a wet Tur-
ban, in the misty cloud.

A colourful finger beautified by the evening
Sun.

The fingernail was just like the new moon,

That created a mesmerising scene.

In one of his travels in Mesopotamia with
Sultan Saladin in the following poem, he
says:

To the Nile

Take it from me a message to the river Nile:

*Let her know, I can never quench my thirst
From Euphrates*

*You can question my heart whether I am
Telling the truth.*

Even if my tears may not be able to show,

Or would not become my honest witness.

*Oh, my love, how many *Baotanists you left
Behind?*

*However, God would not let you kneel down,
Jamil is so sad for your calmness and Patience.*

**(Baotanist, the name of Egyptian Pharaoh's women).*

Qadi Fadil often read this 'Qasidah', lyric :

When the eyes of luck watches over you

Sleep with no fear, as the place of danger
Becomes the place of peace.

*Follow the *phoenix stars, you will find Your-*
self in the web of fortune.

The Orion star becomes your horse and your
Good luck becomes its bridle.

**(Phoenix stars represent good luck, and Orion for*
power.)

The following are a few more of his poems:

A Night of Happiness

We passed the night of happiness that
Matched well with our willing desire

It was a great occasion, far beyond anyone's
Expectation

The night had to be on guard, as the she
Was our only witness.

It was to destroy our happiness by the Cru-
elty of morning light.

In other poems, he says:

The Leisure of the Night

Oh, what a joyful night passed, when we
Were at the mountain feet.

When I tried to narrate it, hardly anyone
Would believe.
I told the night to guard our doors, not let our
Happiness plundered,
As the hands of contempt would be coming,
With the early morning light.

Another of his poems, he says:

With the Eyes of Thinking

*With the eyes of thinking, it was possible to
See.
Her appearance was left on my mind, as I
Woke up in the early morning.
My heart grasped her hand so hard, her
Fingers started bleeding.*

He was born in the town of Escalon in 1135. His father was the head judge of Baysan, therefore, they were called Bayisani. He worked with his father before he travelled to Alexandria [date] with Sultan Saladin. Aumara a Yamani poet wrote about him in his book, *'Nukat Alasaryia'* the puns of ancient words, when he wrote about one of the Fatyimid first minister *'Adil Ibn Salih Ibn Ruzaiq.'*

[Name] worked with Sultan Saladin until he died in 1193. After the Sultan's death, he worked with the Sultan's son, King Aziz Afdal, until Sultan Saif aldin Adel, the brother of Saladin removed him from power and replaced him with his own son, King Mansour in [date].

Qadi al Fadil continued in his work until his death in 1200 in Cairo, Egypt. He was buried in the Karrafa Cemetery, at the Mount Muqatam. On his grave was the inscription, 'Qadi Alfadil as an artistic treasure of the epoch.'

From Ibn Khalikan's biographical dictionary, volume 2
page 111-116

Baha al Din Sinjari 1138 – 1225

Beha Asad Sinjari, was a poet and a doctor in jurisprudence from the 'Shafii' Muslim religious sect. He was renowned for writing essays, prose and 'qasida,' lyrics. He had an original style of writing that he used to earn his living. He often praised Emirs, Sultans and kings for money and gifts. He went far and wide across the Islamic world writing poetry, lyrics, and prose. He was born in Sinjar a town near Mosel, in Kurdish occupied part of Mesopotamia, and died there.

Ibn Khalikan said 'as I was trying to find samples of his writing, I found some in King Ashraf Ayuibid's library in Damascus,' The following is an example of his work:

A Confession of Love

I swear upon the sense of loving you, I never
Had any doubt in my affection

If anyone tells you something in contrary

You should know, that is the one who is
Against our closeness.

The way I feel, is it not enough to show how
Much I think about you?

Is there no justice, or that is not enough for
Recognition?

When you have snapped the connection that
Had brought us together for so long

Was there something happened or it was just
An accident.

Were you against whatever passed, and
Overlooked whatever gone wrong?

Now, it looks so obvious, and to understand
You have changed.

It is so odd for an inflicted slave like me to
Give up with his life's fortunes.

*For someone who is now free from loving
Feeling, then I am ready to leave*

*I put my parents as a ransom for the archer
Whose glances are like arrows.*

*When in his glowing cheeks are showing a
Wealth of youth.*

*In his sparkling eyes are much wealth of
Beauty and so handsome.*

*Now he is going to overlook his own beauty
To risk his life in a volatile sea*

*Nothing else needed to be accomplished in
The science of his virtue and novelty.*

*To obtain fortunes that will protect Kamal al
Din Sharazouri from envious eyes.*

*One can see the letter (Noon) * like a black
Mole distinct with its darkness*

*For me, it has become like the feeling of
Misery and hatred,*

*(noon) in Arabic, it is the equivalent of N in Eng-
lish, that is like a curve open at the top with a
black dot in the middle.

Ibn Khalikan said about Sinjary, '*I have always wanted to tell the truth about anything mentioned in this collection that may mean anything else whatsoever. I would like to be truthful with my conscience; it is not fair deliberately to make any changes for any reason.*'

In the following poems, Sinjary says:

Like A Nymph

Like a nymph, whose curvy slender waist
Shows sweetness and beauty?

Her glances cause temptation, when she let
So many people see

Her moist glistening lips with drinking wine
Reflects the crimson glow of her cheeks

Her charm, sweet and soothing talks would
Be fitting for consolation

For many, when these conciliatory charming
Methods are forbidden.

There is hardly any outlet for anyone to Suc-
ceed.

In another poem he says,

Slender and Sweet

With her wealth of beauty, she was so Slender and sweet

Her captivating glances, invited so many to Meet,

The sparkling lips reflected so often the Blushing glow of her cheeks.

Her charms consoled many souls, would Inflict many into submission,

However, that was still not enough for Anyone's satisfaction.

With drinking tasty wine, we were flying with Merriness.

The wine itself was going to fly,

If it had not been detained, with the froth of Its rousing surface.

Imad al Din Esfahani mentioned this poet,
who he once met, in his book, 'Al Kharida,'
and read him the following poem:

How Surprising

*How surprising when I am on the voyage of
Affluence, but, still I am dying from thirst,
When I am on the beautiful route of my Voyage. But I am still so astonished with Mesmerising scenes such as these.*

Sinjari was born in 1138, and died in 1225, in the town of Sinjar.

From Ibn Khalikan, volume 1, page 196

Buri Taj al Din Ayiubi 1161 – 1183

Buri was the youngest brother of Sultan Saladin Ayiubid. He was a well-known poet during his lifetime. Buri's wounded his knee in the battle of Aleppo, as Saladin's army besieged the town in [date]. He was taken back to Damascus for treatment, but died a few days later. He was a well-known young poet, and in one of his poems he says:

For a Young Maid

Oh, whenever you are around, you display
The art of beauty

I am so sad, wretched, burdened with Dis-
tress or nearly dead

How beautiful that black mole on your rosy
Cheek

Between your eyelashes, mysterious forces
Make me feel so weak.

However I try to be strong, loving you caused
Me so much distress

I am still hoping to grab your hand at least for
Once,

Then I will be relieved so much even if it was
A mistake.

In another poem, he says:

For a Slender maid

*When you have a spear in your hand, It is
Just like your slender waist.*

*Your glances like thrusting spear, which In-
flicted me with pain.*

*You should put away your sword and spear,
In your presence I am so weak*

*So effective are your glances, I am nearly
Perished.*

The day Buri Taj al Din died, [date], Aleppo surrendered to Saladin. In the aftermath of his death, Sultan Saladin said, 'Aleppo wasn't easy to capture, it cost me the life of my brother.'

From Ibn Khalikan's Biographical Dictionary, part 1 page139-140.

Muafaq al Din Erbilli ? – 1189

Muafaq al Din Erbilli was from Erbil. When he was with his family in Bahrain on a commercial visit, he was born there, then called Bahrani, (*Bahrani meant, he was from Bahrain*) as his father was a merchant, who often travelled to Bahrain for commercial voyage.

He was a well know poet and a grammarian in Erbil. He mastered writing prose and poems, and was particularly well-known for his abilities in Greek sciences. He wrote a book about the Greek Euclid Greek mathematics.

He found influence among the desert Arab poets who's works inspired him to begin writing and studying poetry. He became a scholar in creative writing in [date]. He died in Erbil in 1189.

The following examples of his poems:

The Palace of Ghada

*The palace of Ghada has been in distress for
A long time and it is rotting.*

When the travellers pass by, they shed tears,

*Its walls covered with a rusty green layer and
Dark soot.*

*It has decayed with passing years and worn
Out of all its charm.*

*Now, I see nothing left from its merriness; it
Seems all are in ruins.*

All of that have passed, Alas.

*When the grace of God was so plentiful, it
Used to rain down on this place.*

*Now, the dark bunks of cloud in the morning
Often lingers above*

*As if lingers above its soil to unleash tears,
As their chests full of distress.*

*It is instead of my tears to rain on its derelict
Remains when I left.*

*Praise God, may pour his mercy on this
Household, with plenty of wealth and grace.*

*Tell the ones who used to live there, the
Brotherly connections we had, were lost.*

*To leave him alone, but still I love you, for
Your honour and respect.*

*Like a tree used to be so tall, no birds would
Be able to reach your height.*

*When anyone passed, there were guards
Every night.*

*They were always there ready with their
Bleeding spears*

*Whoever's hand reached its branches, Be-
fore snatching the fruits were soon cut From
their armpits.*

*The burden of your honour and defence idle
And tired at the end*

*Then it is easy for the ones, who used to
Look with temptation.*

*There would be no defence when it became
An easy bounty to snatch.*

For your fruitful land, but I would not be
Tempted for a new pasture

In its place, anywhere to reach will be so
Hard.

My God has created in me not to take my
Herd to the height's easy green.

The place where his herd used to be, I have
No hope, in despair I've come seeking help

Helplessness stood before me and made me
Shrink back.

It did not let me arrive; I did not turn up at
Last.

My desire for your love as it started with
Passion

You should not think I will be back;
Experience treated me with a poke in the ay!

Now: if Zain al Din does me a favour, then I*
Have no need for anyone's charity or

Goodness.

Muafaq al Din died on Sunday 21st May 1189 and was buried in Erbil.

*Hajar is a small area or village in Bahrain where his father hosted and used to stay when he was in Bahrain for his commercial trips

*Zain al Din, the governor of Erbil at the time this poem was written.

Ibn Khalikan, part 2 page 172-173

Ziya al Din Ibn Asir 1163 – 1240

Abd al Waheed Shaybani, known as Ibn Asir Jaziri, was a kurdish poet, essayist and historian. He born in Jazira, in North Kurdistan, Mesopotamia. During his childhood, he stayed in Jazeera, but later went to Mosel to start his education. He studied jurisprudence and rhetoric, and discovered a fondness for poetry. He learned off by heart poems by Mutanabi, Abu Tamam and Bahoori who were well known Arab desert poets, and studied their style and method of writing essays.

He studied administration and later worked for Nuraldin Ali Afzal, the son of Sultan Saladin, who took the reign of the Ayiubid Empire, after Sultan Saladin death in 1193. After Nuraldin Afzal lost his power at Damascus, Zainaldin Ibn Asir lost his job and travelled different countries to look for work. He was unsuccessful, and he travelled back to Mosel.

He was the author of a few books about poetry and prose. The following are examples of his poems:

Your wealth

You should invest your wealth that is so
Priceless. This is the choice of a man, who
Owns laws of honesty

For all his ability: style, choice, charm, and
The wealth of creativeness. From his
Childhood, his inventions has continued

On the right path of assertion, has been
Writing poetry.

Ziya al Din, left behind a book about science of administration, within this book many letters to Emirs and leaders in his time. In the following poem, he describes a journey to his leader in a cold weather and torrential rain:

The Passage in the Torrential Rain

*The cloud of rain set up a tent on the land
Like a tunic and a waistcoat. No chance,
One could not stay sheltered, as the valleys
Between the hills were filled up with rain.*

*Each like a pool filled up and drilled the
Stomach of earth, carried soil, and formed
Streams and rivers. I feel as though it has
Been imitating generosity of our king's Offer-
ing.*

*Just like the torrential rain, your faithful Ser-
vant kept pleading with God's forgiveness
For making such a comparison.*

*Between the two different offerings, if that is
Against God's law, he is well aware of the
Difference: the clouds that fills up valleys,
With the gifts of man ready at his divan.*

*The roses that is charity's produce, which
Exterminates by the summer heat. Just like
The fruit, that autumn season wants its life to
Cease.*

*That is not possible to compare with the
Amir's wealth of jewels.*

When the God's generous intention of the
Spring, as flocks of birds eat and graze, in
His lush green and well watered plains.

Now, your servant, on his way, burdened
With mud and rain. The sky continues its Of-
fering like our faithful friend; until his hands
Get tired to carry plentiful gifts are so many.

But your faithful servant is now suffering from
The pain caused by a thunderbolt more than
Taking from a brandished sword. During this
Rain, he often tried to stop and wait,

I will offer my salute; in the battle of travelling
I am often caught.

One of his friends, a poet called Hajeery,
heard about his poem and his experience in
his travels, he wrote:

Travels with Pain

How that is with pain his lips are so cold!

I am crying with passion and sympathy.

I complain against the one who blames me

For loving him.

Ibn Mstawfi highly regarded him in his book,
'*The History of Erbil.*'

He was born in Jazira, North Mesopotamia,
in November 1163 and died in 1239 in Baghdad, when he was sent on a mission by the
governor of Mosel to meet Caliphate Abbasid
of Baghdad.

Ibn Khalikan, volume 3 page 541 - 549.

Emad al Din Esfahani 1125 – 1201

Muhamad Saful Din Faraj Muhamad Nafisal Din, known as Emad al Din Esfahani, was the secretary and advisor of Sultan Saladin. He studied law at Nizamyia College in Baghdad. He also studied prose and poetry, and wrote essays on science and the law of administration.

As a child, he came to Baghdad and was successful in his quest for science and knowledge and became reputable. He gained praise and reached high places in Iraq and Syria, and eventually became the secretary, minster, and advisor of Sultan Saladin Ayiubi.

He was a well know essayist and a poet, and the following are some of his poems:

To Abdul Rahman

*With the hammering of horses' hooves dust
Rose like the hill of sand*

*It made the sky dark, but your presence has
Brought sunlight*

*Oh, goodness protects me; let him stay Mr
Abdul Rahman*

*I would not be scared, no more from the
Sharp eagles' beaks, and tearing claws of
Contempt.*

Here, Emad al Din wrote on Alfaidl's trip to
'Haj', the pilgrimage at Mecca:

Alfadil's Hadj

*Happiness for Hajeer and Hajoon, for the
One who is clever and aware*

*When his pride reaches stars, his existence
Glows darkness of the sky!*

*Happiness for the gathering at Kaaba, as he
Is the 'kaab'* of generosity*

*From his offering shows the way of Right-
eousness*

*It is such a joy for Abd al Raham's abode,
From his honourable site towards Hatim*

*For whom would break the poverty's back,
When he appears like a Pyramid*

*From the sanctity of the place so great when
The birds flying over and are guided to the
Water of Zemzem.*

*For the ocean, he is the ocean of science on
The dry land with his God's grace so plenty*

*Qaiss who returned to Ukass himself, Qaiss
Who returned with religiousness.*

Praise for Kaaba, that he visited as the
Source of wealth, and himself the source of
Offering, and sanctity, as he is going towards
The emblem of prayer and respect.

For the one who is the source of plenty and
To the centre of the world who does farewell.

Ibn Khalikan criticised him for the use of Qaiss in this poem and says, 'it should have been "*Unass*" as the source of knowledge and the leader of prayers.'

He worked for the governor of Wasit, in South Iraq, a few years before he was employed by Saladin in [date]..

When the governor of Wasit died, all the employees of the previous governor were arrested and imprisoned. Emad al Din was one of those imprisoned in June 1165.

One of his friends, the poet Adudd al Din Ruwaisa, upon hearing the news of his arrest was not pleased and contacted Khalifa Mustanjid, the Abbasid Caliph in Baghdad, and informed him about Emad al Din's imprisonment and pleaded for his release in the following poem:

For Imad al Din

*Tell the Mukhtar of Caliph, why the Impris-
onment of Wali? You may show Sympathy
for the one who is your faithful Servant.*

*When the cloud stops the rain, and there is
No rain anymore, is it not possible with
Prayers' pleading to clear the way for the
Freedom of raining?*

When Khalifa received this letter, he gave
the order to release Emad al Din from prison.

A few years later, Emad al Din became secretary of Saladin until sultan's death in 1993.
He became jobless, poor and started writing
about his memoir and his life. He wrote a
book titled the *Glitter of *Sham,* and wrote
about his years with Saladin.

*Syria

Ibn Khalikan met a man who used to be in
touch with Emad al Din in the later period of
his life. He often visited him, and said,
*'whenever I went to see him, he used to read
these lines*:

*'I am coming to your house like a guest,
Where is he? Can you let me know where
The master of the house is?*

*My friend does not recognise me anymore,
They are all dead, the ones who I used to
Know.'*

Emad Ad Din was born on 6th July 1125, in Esfahan, East Persia, and died in Damascus on 5th June 1201. He was buried in the cemetery of *'al Sufi bab al Nasra.'*

Mukhtar is a Khalifa officer in charge, *walli* the governor's deputy who was Emad al Din in prison. Caliph: the Abbasid Caliph of Baghdad

Kaab, is the centre of gathering of pilgrims. *Zemzam*, the holly water of a well in Mekka Hajeer & Hajoon and Unass places in Saudi Arabia

From Ibn Khalikan's book, volume 2 page 301- 306

Ibn Asroon 1099 – 1189 'the Kurdish judge of Damascus.'

Ibn Asroon was born in February 1099 in Hakari, South Kurdistan, in Mosel's Kurdish region. He studied jurisprudence, poetry, and prose, and became an able poet, essayist and a writer. In his youth he studied under guidance of many known scholars, amongst them: Murtada Sharazouri a Kurdish scholar, Saruji, son of Abbas Mzrati, Mahani, Kurdish scholar in Baghdad. He travelled to Wasit, '*a town South of Baghdad'* when Fariqi, a Kurd, was the Judge of the town.

Ibn Asroon became a tutor in Mosel at the time of the Zanjid dynasty in 1154 and then travelled to Aleppo in Syria. He wrote books on jurisprudence, and a book on the foundation of Islamic law. He travelled to Damascus, and became the Judge of Damascus when Kamal al Din Sharzouri left his post as a judge in 1174. A few well known writers in Damascus wrote about him, such as Emad al Din Esfahani and Abu Tahir Askandarni, who wrote and published a book about the history of the Damascus.

Ibn Asroon was a poet and the following are a few examples of his writing:

I aspire

*I aspire for the long life, which looks as if the
Hours are going towards the final stroke so
Fast, as they pass. When it is showing me
The podium, where my coffin would be. Am I
Waiting to pass the sad hours of my misery?
Until I spend all the hours of my life's left of
Being.*

In the following poem, he says:

For Love

*I always hope to see my love, although I
Have no doubt I would have to leave her so
Early in a hurry on the horse of my honour.*

*Our lives will end when the time comes at
Last. We will not feel the bitter taste of losing
Each other. You asked me how I was since
The last time we met. God will protect you
From my heart's desire; I sensed when I left*

*Tears of sadness have been streaming
Down, ever since always every day of life.
For my eyes have never been acquainted
With sleep until we will meet again.*

*The times which passed, they would never
Turn back. There are times that we could
Never wait for anymore. Life is the days and
Times resulted in the adding of the two:*

*The first keeps decreasing and the other is
Adding up life's hours to the final destiny.*

Ibn Asroon was the judge in the sultan Saladin era for a long time. In his last ten years of his life, he went blind with cataract, but on the order of the sultan, he kept his post until he died in October 1189 in Damascus, and was buried in the school's backyard that was founded in his name.

Ibn Khalikan, volume 1 page 32–36

King Zahir Ghazi 1173 – 1216

King Ghazi, the son of Sultan Saladin Ayiubi, was hnown as Zahir al Gazi. He was the King of Allepo, and a chevalier and a clever Emir who fought face to face against Richard the First, the king of England. He often hosted scientists, artists, poets, and scholars for educational and esoteric discussions. His father, Sultan Saladin, bestowed upon him the town of Aleppo in 1186, as he removed his brother Saifaldin Adel from Aleppo and gave him Kirak, another state of the Aiyubid Empire, in Egypt.

As Ibn Khalikan narrates, there were many stories about this young king, his wisdom and maturity in his post. He was born in Cairo in May 1173, when his father, Sultan Saladin was the King of Egypt for eight years. He died in Aleppo castle in October 1216, and was buried in the Castle. One of his tutors was Shehab al Din Toghrol Atabek, an Armenian, who stayed with King Ghazi from his childhood until his death.

It was a strange coincident, that the date he was put on power was the same date he died, in October 1216.

About this king a poet whose name is Abu Wafa Sharf al Din Raji Ismael, Qasim Asadi al Hilli wrote a ballad about his death when he praised and described his qualities, and also praised his two sons, Sultan Muhamed Malik and Ahmad Salih, the leader of Ain al Tab in Syria. In his poem, he says:

Ask the destiny

*Ask the destiny with a promise and a
Warning when applied its command, who is
The one that caught him with its hook and
Beak?*

*Reprimand it I will not accept the calamity it
Brought. Whether it turns away, annoyed
And blames me for what I say.*

*Oh, God protect me! From my astonishment,
When I turned my face to the sky of glory,
With all its stars dim! Oh, what has
Happened?*

*The Brightness of Aleppo changed to misery
In such darkness! Is that reality? Sanctity
Has backed off the warrior Ghazi!*

*The assistant of Ghazi son of Joseph was
Not being cared for. Is that respect of the
Amir and his faithfula, when marched without
His highness?*

*Alas! It is very true when the day's language
Of your greatness was abandoned.*

*The heaven's glory of your achievement like
A precious carpet has been taken and put
Away. It was disappeared just like your
Wealth and achievement.*

*Who can tell me more about his mountains
Of glory? Has it gone down in the ground
And buried all its columns?*

*Oh, was it, with a stroke or a heart attack he
Collapsed? Yes! The mount that stood with
No obstacle was hit with an earthquake*

*Has his right and left shoulders hit with such
A strong gust wind of destiny and shivered?
His ocean of grace, and charity like
Enormous waves, now dried up!*

*When their waves used to reach furthest
Borders of earth, it erupted at the hands of
Destiny. Oh, its vengeful sword brandished
With such hatred*

*For the greatness of his glory, that may snap
Sharp edges of the sword! Then the rain of
His grace and charity now disappeared!*

When so often cascaded with the stream of
Generosity. The man who used always live
With aspirations, but now has nothing to say.

How can we have any sense of happiness
Other than the fact we lost son of Joseph?
Is that because so much he desired and
Succeeded was not enough?

His horses did not stop at the country of
Plunder when there was so much on offer.
The green pasture is now so mean for
Grazing, at the frowned face of destiny.

The empty bags of his saddled horses are
Not ornamented when they trot. The Emir
Who put everyone under the porch of law,
And protected them from grudges and harms
To reach their abode.

How many tall and proud castles kneeled
Down when captured before his sword!

So many poor and lonely he protected from
The enemy army's insult.

Now, I can see the Empire's throne so
Empty, can anyone tell me and let me know,

*Where can I find out who that is, the next so
Great?*

*If anyone would question me, why I shed so
Many tears? My heart might be able to give
Reply with a deep sigh With so many
Wounds I am inflicted they may perish my
Soul.*

*With the waling-cry when women in
Mourning! Did he give up fighting before he
Saw the blade of his sword worn out and
Bland? Before his army failed to return or
Scared and hesitated in the battle.*

*Were the army of his horsemen had been
Defeated and perished in facing the enemy?
This is not like revenge that the enemies
Would inflict, in a day's fighting back*

*When did his chivalries lost, and run back in
The dark cloud dust of defeat?*

*Oh, your death clothed me in the dark tunic
Of mourning. Is there any consolation to put
Away my costume of mourning?*

*I was one of your faithful servant in the
Shade of enormous orchards of your
Victories and gains.*

*When the ocean of generosity provided me,
Your generosity was plenty.*

*You were the pride of my closeness and
Honour. I am not only praising you for your
Generosity, but this is for your phenomenal
Virtues of knowledge and greatness.*

*I do feel like to be honoured permission to
Come to you, why it is not possible to grant
Me that honour again?*

*I was never amongst the ones who the guard
Would stop them from meeting you. Oh, for
The day we lost you, as if time stopped, but
Was it not a total eclipse?*

*How can it be possible the sword of your
Commands is now so bland? How the
Chivalry of generosity did trip over when you
Were the worrier?*

*Oh, Ghazi when the rain of your offering
Dried up for the community of orphans. Then*

*Your generous rain would never quench the
Year's need of rain.*

*Who can now lead and become the head,
The Emirs like you capable and brave?*

*For the protection of the comforted courts of
Wealth, that was under your mighty
Command.*

*You now have left me, put arms around my
Neck; you presented me with peace of our
Enemies. When this disaster inflicted me, it
Is just like uttered words of mockery.*

*Let the dark cloud of the early mourning pour
Down its rain on your grave, and the evening
Rain to quench the flame of your glowing
Instinct.*

*Let the glint of your grace overcome the
Darkness of night with the brightness of your
Greatness. Now, in the flourishing youth of
Emir Mohamed I am looking forward to what
I expect*

*Like the brightness of early morning to lead
Us on the right way.*

A proud hero like his father, his head would
Be high with no equals

Like his father made all his enemies
Subdued, that showed him ways of
Greatness.

After the death of King Ghazi, his son, Muzafar Mohamed replaced his father with the
surname of King Aziz. He was born in Aleppo
in April 1204, and died in Aleppo November
1236.

Sharf al Din Hilli, was a well-known poet. He
was born in November 1230 died in Damascus in July 1274. he was buried in Narnj
Mosque, in Musalari, outside Damascus.

Ibn Khalikan, volume 2 page 443-446

Ibn Saaty 977 – 1028

Abu Hasan Harduz, with the surname Ba-
hadin, was known by son of Saati, was
known as the leader and tutor of a number of
poets. He had two collections of poems, one
of them known as *'Muqatati Neel,'* (Oasis of
the Nile).

Following are a few examples of his poems:

A Trip in spring

*We pulled up in the heights' newly dressed
Plain, it offered new pastures to the soul.*

*With the new shade, I admired the beauty of
This place:*

The infant flowers perfumed the air.

My friend swore: look!

*The orange evening' sky so clear. The Sil-
ver-crystal streams are edged with the soft
And silky green costumes.*

*The blushed Antamis flowers as if exhibited
White petals for kissing.*

*They were trying to hide their white beads
With lips and cheeks, while so many Specta-
tors held back with anticipation.*

In the following poem he says,

For a Young Lady

*Oh, for such a beauty of your neck, it does
Not need any jewels or necklace.*

*In desperation for your smile, I am almost
Losing my head.*

*On the tips of your eye lashes a string of
Colourful beads. Do you really want to put
Them round your rousing chest?*

*I am just like the light evening breeze; you
Should not fret over my presence.*

For your slender figure has no ill effect.

Emad al Din, the minister of Sultan Saladin
tried to meet Ibn Saati, as he was known for
his beautiful lyrics and poetry. The quality of
his poetry and prose had no equal. On another occasion Emad al Din said,

*'When Saladin returned from Egypt on one of
his trips, his army camped outside Hums, Ibn
Saati came to visit Sultan and informed that
he was the poet who wrote about Rusaziq,
'the Fatimid's first minister Ruzaiq,' and he
wrote a poem for Sultan Saladin.'*

His poems were known to be full of beauty
and tenderness, as Ibn Khalikan said,

*'his son informed me about the date of his
death in April 1028. He lived over fifty-one
years, and he was buried at the Muqatam
Mountain in Egypt; and he was born in Damascus.'*

Ibn Assad arrived in Egypt, and met the firts
minister of the Fatimid dynasty and wrote a
poem, which its lines ended with the letter
K.*

After he settled in the town of Hums in Syria, he became professor and was given the name of 'Himsi' as it meant someone from Hums.

*(this poem is on page 658, volume 1 of Ibn Khalikan's book)

His name Saati meant the watchmaker. The Antamis flower petals like lips and the white colour is the reference to colour of teeth.

Ibn Khalikan, volume 2 page, 328,-329

Ibn Asadi Mosli 1125 – 1185

Abdulla Assad Ali, was the son of Essa
Dahani. He was from a merchant family from
Mosel, who immigrated to the town of Hums
and lived there until he died. He was known
as a judge and a poet. His poems are known
in the range of a high quality. He was born in
Mosel and immigrated to Egypt with the hope
of reaching to the Fatimid ruler Ruzaiq. He
had to leave his wife when he left for Egypt
and wrote a poem about it, as it says:

The Woman in Despair

The woman in despair, was shedding tears

With the hope of stopping me from leaving

'You are leaving me as a result of you
Ignorance.' She said,

She was trying in vain, but I did not listen.
Seeing her shedding tears wounded my
Heart.

Her sadness brought together all the ones
Who felt sad for my leaving. When the
Caravan was ready:

'Look, they are all crying for you.

Who will come to give me a hand, when you
Left?' Lady said.

God will. Abu Ubaidulla, the leader.

There is one whose generosity so plenty, you
Should not fret over your poverty.

The one who promised me, like the rain of
Yalidaz, his generous grace so plenty.

The mighty God will rain on his household so
Much grace.

Katib Emad Ad Din, secretary of Saladin Aiyubi, mentioned his name in his book, '*Al Kharida*.' When he was in Iraq, he tried to meet him, as Emad al Din heard about his poems which were known for their lyrical beauty. What added to the uniqueness of his poetry was that the poet's lips pronunciation that added uniqueness to the quality of his reading.

(Yalidaz, a mythical lover which from distress of being left behind, she turned to a star in the sky, in Greek mythology).

When the governor of the town heard about this poem, he promised to provide for the woman who he left behind in Mosel.

Another of his poems:

I told the woman, the one who did not reply
To my greeting, as for religious reasons.
Why you are so senseless, as if you drain
My blood?

You should not think, I would come
Whenever you want, or before your return,
Myth of beauty.

As if God has used all powers of urgency!
Has it not become like a burden, to give me
Your hand of sympathy? I would dearly love
You, however my destiny might be.

In another poem, he says,

How dear that girl whose lips stung by a bee,
That hurt and disturbed the repose of her
Beauty

The swollen pouting lips that God has
Created for kissing

Her mouth has become like a honeycomb,
And her lips' moisture for honey.

Ibn Saati's poems known with tenderness and beauty, as Ibn Khalikan says, 'his son informed me with the date of his death in April, 1028, he lived fifty one years and twelve days, he was buried at the feet of the Muqatam Mountain, and was born in Damascus.

Ibn Saati meant, the watch mender, Antamis flower's whitness is similar to the whiteness of teeth.

Ibn Khalikan, Volume 1 page 36-39.

Ibn Mstawfi Erbilli 1039 – 1169

Ahmad Mubarak Mauhub Ghunaim Laqmi, was born in Erbil. He was one of the high ranking officials of the city, referred to as 'Raies' the Leader. He often looked after well known visitors of the city who came on official visits; he paid them visits, invited them to his home, and gave them presents. He was especially courteous towards scientists, poets, and well known personalities.

He was known as an able poet and a prose writer, who was acquainted with philosophy, Arabic grammar. He was an able mathematician, and administrator. He worked for many years on writing and collecting information on the History of Erbil, and known as the Erbil Historian.

He wrote books on art & literature, one of those was on Abu Tamam and Mutanabi poems. One of his books was the detailed analysis of Al Zamashkary's juriprudence. He wrote a book on Siret al Sanyia about science of administration. He wrote another book named 'Abu Qumash' a literary analysis and art criticism.

As Ibn Khalikan said, *'whenever he had well known guests in Erbil, he often showed them samples of his literary works from his books.'*

As Ibn Khalikan also said, *'he was often present listening to reading extracts of his work.'*

Ibn Khalikan often used his books in his research to write his well known book on the life of Known personalities in the history of Islam, *'Wafayati Ayan u Anbei al Zaman.'* 'History of the known Personalities who died and the News of the Epoch.'

One of his books he left behind was a collection of his poems.

The following are a few lines of his poems:

A night with Love

*For the whole night I was awake to compare
Her beauty with the moon. I wrapped my
Arms around her waist for the most length of
Time. I was offered happiness and the
Happiest was my night*

*When my love blamed me for so long, but I
Was yet not satisfied. Even with her angry
Looks, her face seemed so sweet. That
Night became so wonderful, just like a*

Wonderful meeting feast.

*We had to hide from the jealous eyes, as
Their intention was with contempt. So*

Graceful was her warm touch, she often

Clung to my neck

*So many aspects of her beauty especially
Her slender curvy waste: her elegant*

*Colourful dancing, was so graceful her every
Single step. So enticing her tender grooves,
Like medicines for ailments.*

*Pride almost stopped me, as I blushed from
My naughty moves. But she still was in my
Arms and kept kissing her warm cheeks.*

If it was not for our coupled breathing, my
Gasping would have been heard. The
Jealous morning was coming, when the night
Was already aware. When the vengeful
Morning came, it soon confirmed our
Despair.

In another poem he says,

With your dark olive colour so wonderful that
Embellished the art of your beauty. What is
The benefit of the white skin? When the
Sword's fatal part is white.

Whenever it is brandished inflicts pain and
Killing.

Now, you may clearly see my suffering?

Ibn Khalikan said: 'w*henever he had well known guests in Erbil, he often showed them and offered them samples of his literary art works and his books*'. One of the books he left behind was a collection of his poems.

Ibn Mstawfi left Erbil after the Turkish Tatarist massacre and occupation of Erbil in 1237, when when most of the Erbil population were massacred. He died in Mosel in 1239 and buried in the Jahasha cemetery.

From Ibn khalikan's biographical dictionary volume 2 page 556-562.

Ibn Babek 1060 – 1120

 Abd al Samad Mansoor, son of Hasan
Babek, was a well known poet with beautiful
lyrics. As Ibn Khalikan says,
*'I have seen his written works in three
editions of poetry, essays, and prose.'*

He travelled extensively, and met many
leaders, scholars, and poets.

The following are some examples of his
poems:

The Atlas Girl

*The mythic beauty of Atlas girl called me with
Her steady steps.
Soon with the glow of her presence, the
Night's darkness disappeared.
Was it the morning light, or the glow of her
Beautiful eyes?
Rays of light had gone through and torn
Bunks of cloud.
She came with quivering glances, like a
Scared desert deer. Despite the night's
Darkness her beauty showed everywhere.
Her power of tender beauty, so strong had
No equal and carefree.
I had my share in the purple wine, when the
Evening stars were in view.*

*On the surface of her wine-cup, I shared my
Passion for romance.
Like the sharp arrows of infliction, may have
Caused bleeding tears.
If that was directed at anyone, blood would
Spill everywhere
When the scarf removed from her face, her
Shyness was quite clear.*

However, with the taste of sweet wine, all
Barriers soon cleared.
So masterfully was managed, by man's
Desire and passion
We passed the night with care, as all secrets
Were well retained
Our loving feeling continued until our aims
Were well understood.
Like a thirsty morning pheasant, was
Heading to the water spring
When the grieving pigeon took refuge, was
Lonely on the bouncing tree branch.
The maid withdrew with her plight from
Drinking so much wine
And raised her hand for a good bye, then
Said, 'no worry I am fine.'

In other poems, he says:

My Dear Friends

My dear friends: pour me a glass of wine; let
The sparkles lighten up the darkness of the
Night.
So long as the glittering bubbles remain in
Suspense.

I shiver with fear for losing my friend, who
Might not be able to have a sip.
No one would deny that when the dawn
Would show clear truthfulness.
For showing, her true appearance in the
Broad day light that is two-faced.

In another poem, he says:

The Breeze

When the breeze passed by tenderly,
I was dreading my toiling pains.
As I sighed with such a distress, as though,
The morning breeze sensed what I thought.

Ibn Babek died in Baghdad in 1120

Ibn Khalikan, volume 2 page 145-146

Ibn Hajeer Erbilli 1075 – 1125

Fadil Eissa Sinjari, was the son of Ibrahim Jibril Khumrtakin Tashtekin Erbilli. He was born in Erbil, known as Hajeery. He was a soldier, as his father was in the service of the Erbil governor.

He left many beautiful poems behind. The style of his short poems consisted of couplets, or two line verses. He had a collection of prose and essays published, as Ibn Khalikan has seen his works, and said,

'His ability in writing was with tender flows and beauty in all his written works, one of his written works titled,' "Qana wa Qana".

His published works referred to by the following German source:

Freytag's Darste ung der Arabisclen Verskunst. its translated as:

'Art of intermediate Arabic verse'

As in the following verse says:

Being with You

*Oh, being with you I so much desire
God is well aware of my pain of separation.*

*I have been left with nothing from the Happi-
ness. You have to send me a letter of Consolation.*

*Therefore, I may die before your letter would
Arrive. I want to make sure, if you were Happy and not in need.*

*You should let me know and make me Reas-
sured, I am so desperate for your news.*

As Ibn Khalikan says,Ibn Hajeer, was a
friend of his brother, he knew this poet, and
he sometimes read his poems to him.' He
died in Erbil in 1222 or 1223.

Volume 2 page, 434-437.

Ibn Mushir Mosli 1197 – 1248

Ali Wafa Saad, was the son of Hasan Ali Abdul Hamid Ahmed Mushiri, from Mosel, with the surname of Muhadab. He was an able poet, with a connection in the government, and held high positions in employment. He wrote essays and poems with a focus on people in power and Caliphs. Ibn Khalikan said, 'I have seen some of his essays and poems in two editions. In one of his published works, where his place of birth mentioned.'

He was born in the town of Amedi, 'Amadyia,' in the Hakari area In South Kurdistan, in 1197.

His style of writing was similar to his contemporary Suruji's poems.

Once he wrote this poem to a known leader of his time when he was ill in bed:

To your Highness

When you do suffer and complain from pain,
All the earth is sad, plighted with suffering,
From the East to the West.

You are like the heart of the epoch.
When the heart is not healthy and not at rest,
The body cannot be content.

In another poem, when the poet meets Ibn
Khalikan himself, he reads the following:

The Language of Tears

Within the language of my tears,
All secrets of my passion were well known, I
Could not hide from anyone my sincere
Intention.

God was the right witness, as I was not
Aware of you leaving, whether the pigeons of
The valley flew away so happily or with the
Rhythm of a sad tune.

I was thinking with anger when your caravan
Was ready, I enquired with the wind to tell
Me, how your art of secrecy was so well-
Managed?

When sadness still lingered between my
Closed ribs, your passionate love was no
Relief, as for such a long waiting in despair it
Could never be ceased.

Ibn Mushiri died in July 1248, but in Emad al Din's book titled, '*Al Kharida*' the date of his death is 1251.

Ibn Khalikan, volume 2 page 326-328
Kamal al Din Sharazouri 1098 – 1176

Abdulla Ahmed Qasim Sharazuri, was called with the surname of Kamal al Din. He studied jurisprudence with Asad Al Din Mahani, *'the Kurdish scholar, mentioned on page 189, volume 1 of Ibn Khalikan.'* He also studied Islamic tradition with Muhamed Khamisi Mosley, 'from Mousl.' He was born in Mosel in 1098.

Kamal Al Din was the 'Qadi' the judge of Mosel, established the Shafi College and the *Ribat* convent in Mosel.

Attabek, the governor of Mosel, made him the head of his envoy to the Abbasid Khalifa, in Baghdad.

When there was a conflict between Turkish Emirs, resulting in the governor of Mosel's removal from his post, he was arrested with his brother, as he was the judge employed by the previous establishment. They were imprisoned until the news reached the Abbasid Khalifa of Baghdad; and he sent a message to the new governor of Mosel to release them from prison. He was still under house arrest until the Emir of Mosel died a few years later.

After the governor of Mosel died in [date], he was freed from the house arrest, and was sent by the new governor of Mosel to Syria 1156 to work for Nuraldin Zangi, the Turkish king of Syria.

In 1160 Kamal al Din became the head judge of Damascus and Syria. He appointed his son and his nephew as judges of two towns in Syria, and was the head of the King's administration of the Zanjid establishment. His son Muhi al Din became his deputy and the judge of Aleppo.

The Zanjid king often sent Kalam al Din to Baghdad as his envoy to meet the Abbasid Khalifa, where he stayed as the head of the Zanjid administration until the king's death, and Sultan Saladin took over the Kingdom of Syria. He left his post and went back to Mosel. He was replaced by Ibn Asroon.

Kamal al Din often established schools and charity centres in Damascus, Nasibin and Mosel.

He was a known essayist and poet. The following are some of his poems Ibn Khalikan managed to obtain from one of his relatives in Damascus:

I was on my way to you

I was on my way coming to you when only
The stars of the sky were aware.
The coming morning was still so far away.
As if my heart was left wounded, imprisoned
Caged in my chest. My only thoughts were
Towards the East, there was no thinking if I
Was taking risks
I was on the way and was toiling hard to
Escape, with aspiration to catch up, and to
Meet you again.

In another poem he wrote to his son far
away:

I am sending my letters

*I am sending many letters in the form of an
Army, which consists of many longing and
Loving desire.
When I am thinking of you, I am in a conflict,
Alas, that is just like wishful thinking.*

*With my hope, I am trying to slow down and
Far from oncoming of the following morning.
Travelling through such a stressful night, so
Many episodes I have seen.*

*I disparately tried to hide flames that were so
Resolute to consume me.
In my longing for support, only stars left to
Reach.
When the sunrise barred my vision and the
Prospect of another morning
The calamity snatched away my fortune with
The strong gripping fist of sunlight.*

Kamal al Din died in Mosel in 1176, and was buried at the Sharzuri Cemetery.

Before his death he suggested that his nephew Fadil Qasim Ibn Yahyia replace him as the Judge of Mosel, with the permission of Sultan Saladin, but after a while, he was involved in a few conflicts with other judges of Syria, and was removed from his post and was replaced by another Kurdish judge named Ibn Asroon.

Ibn Khalikan, volume 2 page 648 - 649.

Ibn Amedi 'Qadi' the Judge 1157 – ?

Yousif Ahmed Abdulla, Husein was from the family of Jafari Amedi. He was born in Wasit / Kut in South Iraq, from a Kurdish family from Amed, a well known family of scholars, essayists, poets, and scientists.

He studied jurisprudence in Baghdad with his tutor Abu Talib Ibn Mubarak (1) at a school called the *Gate of Mazaj* in Baghdad. He obtained his certification in mathematics to become a tutor and an essayist, and he was an accomplished poet. In 1027 he became the judge of Wasit

His poems well known in the area and the following are a few examples of his poetry:

The Passion of Love

*The praise of my lover reminds me of a
Garden, like an orchard that has been well
Looked after and watered.*

*When inhaling the gentle breeze and
Whispered, was puzzled when heard her
Voice. Just like the sound of Bulbul that
Awakens the broken heart, to stack up layers
Of increased pain.*

*That dismisses from one's conscience all
Honesty, as it triggers the pain of lingered
Longing. The longing renews sadness, to
Shed tears for the passionate romance.*

*The days had already passed; even when
The loving feeling had not elapsed.*

*His friends think, he failed, just like a
Mountain that was in pain and wailing when
Going down under the burden of the lost love
And collapsed.*

You should not think, to give up with love, the
Desire and devotion you carried became like
A heavy burden. How can you forget and
Consider it passed?

Never shrink of being wise and reconsider
Your resolve, as you reached the summits of
Attraction. It was for you when the weeping
Willows on hilltops began to shiver in the
Breeze and danced.

They were, assured with seeing your beauty
And loving contention, when you appeared.

 As you generously showed willingness to
Give your frequent glances to the deer of the
Desert. When the most precious object, that
Was there before the eyes of the stag.

As you are moaning and falling ill with pain of
Love and the loss of sleep. I should never
Have rest at night if I do not gain your desire
To show me devotion and kindness.

They were the cheats, the ones who
Watched over us, with tears, my wailing
Cries, and loss of wisdom.

*Is that possible for any mythical story of
Love? Some people may get angry with me
For being so sad, but they should never have
Deprived me of your love.*

*Many had a belief; I would not be able to
Stand it, but I never considered what they
Say, when they tell you I only want you for
Your beauty.*

*It's so odd, beauty is nothing if does not
Trigger the willing desire of love. You are
The only one, from all the loving feeling of
The world. None of those who I know are
Honest, and they never possess your wealth
Of beauty.*

As Ibn Khalikan said, 'he was the poet who was known as one of the best for his ability in creative writing and tender style of his poetry.'

Amongst all his contemporary poets, Gazi *(mentioned on page 138, volume one).* Another writer called, Arajani*, (mentioned on page 138 volume one of Ibn Khalikan's work).*

Ibn Khalikan pointed out that there are two persons mentioned with the name Ibn Amedi, one of them is Ibn Amedi Qadi, which is different from this one who is a poet.

Ibn Khalikan, page 329- 331.

Saifadin Adil 'the King' 1145 –1218 (brother of Sultan Saladin)

Abu Bakr Muhamed shukr Aiyubi, son of Shadi, son of Marwan, with the surname Saifaldin Adil, was the King of the Ayiubid Empire. He travelled to Egypt in 1169 after Saladin and his uncle Shierko were there, when Nur al Din Mahmoud, the Zanjid King of Syria sent them with the intention to bring down the Fatimid Kingdom. As Sultan Saladin established his power, after his uncle, Shierko' sudden death, Shierko became the first minister of the Fatamid King, Al Adid. When Saladin took over from the Fatimid King, he faced significant opposition in Egypt; and he needed his brothers Turansha and Saifadin to support him to establish the Ayiubid power in Egypt. Saladin, with his brothers Turansha and Saifaldin, defeated the Nubis, and the Armenian oppositions who strongly supported Al Adid, the Fatimid king of Egypt.

Saifadin joined his elder brother Turansha, and led a huge army to defeat the crusaders armies who thought there was a chance and

came to occupy Egypt when the Fatimid
Kingdom was ended by Sultan Saladin. But
they were defeated under the leadership of
Turanshah and Saifuldin, after the victory of
the Battle of Dumyat; they marched about
100,000 Ayiubid Empire's army, the biggest
in the history of Islam in Cairo.

When Sultan Saladin returned to Syria as the
Zanjid King died, he marched back with his
army to end the Zanjid Kingdom's rule in
Damascus, that was when Saifaldin was left
in charge of Egypt and several times defeated uprising of the Egyptian oppositions.

 After eight years of siege, Aleppo surrendered to Saladin, and Saifldin returned to
Syria, to become the Emir of the city, until he
was removed in 1186, and was sent to the
Castle of Kirak, where he was was replaced
by Saladin's son King Zahir al Ghazi.

Saifadin backed the establishment of the Ay-
iubid dynasty and his brother Sultan Saladin.
He gained power after Saladin died in 1193
as Saladin sons could not control the Ayiubid
Empire because of their internal conflicts.
Saifaldin gradually regained power and took

over from Saladin's sons and led the Empire for approximately twenty years. He reoccupied all the territories which were lost after Saladin's death. Under his leadership, the Ayiubid dynasty flourished and many parts of the Empire run by his sons from Yemen, Saudi Arabia, Mesopotamia, Syria, Lebanon, Egypt, North Africa to Afghanistan.

The well known Arab poet Ibn Unain from Kuffa often praised King Saifaldin Adil, and the following are a few examples of his poems:

For Saifaldin Adil, the Ayiubid King

*He has numerous sons, each in a different
Country. They are always ready to fight at
The head of their armies.*

*Each one has a bright face with optimism like
A full glowing moon. When during the battle
Are ready, like lions with unflinching heroism.*

*With their glittering blades, that lightens the
Dusty darkness of the battlefield. With
Winning resolve accomplish victory as they
Capture the surrendered maids.*

*For your purity of faith and your distinct
Original race, there is no comparison in
Valour that would relinquish so much
Happiness.*

*Who would be able to attract so much
Attention to astonished glances or gaze;
When your army's horses are not yet
Quenched by the crystal water streams, until
The streams turned red by the spilled blood
Of the battlefield.*

*When they are pressed and hurried into the
Thick of the battle; and are never in a hurry*

Into the inviting glow of comfort and
Hospitaity.

The King Adil's reign was known for peace, prosperity, and equality throughout his kingdom. There was an abundance of prose and poetry written in admiration of the King's achievements, as is seen in the following poem:

The Laws of Adil the King

*That is how the laws of Adil, the King of
Justice so well-known, the fame of his
Kingdom spread all over the countries and
Regions.*

*The king of goodness, what are those he
Achieved? As he established law in every
Region, to be like unequalled heaven.*

*When the law of his kingdom released like
The free flow of the streams. His justice
Would make the hungry wolves pass the day
And night with pain of hunger, even when the
Brown deer were so plenty for everyone to
See.*

*It was not conceivable for any unbeliever to
Have doubt, and not to be able to realise.
Who would dare not to respect the King Abu
Bakir's clever and firm authority?*

*His laws so straight like the smooth blade of
His sword that became the icon of pride and
Victory.*

*On the metal surface of his sword, was
Clearly shown the might of his enormous
Patience.*

*His praises were not forged in any cultural
Banter, or any vulgar or contrite
exaggeration.*

*He is so much above other kings of his era
With no equals. Look in the books about the
Greeks and Persian Kings.*

*Whenever there was confusion and disorder
Anywhere, the power of our king was well in
Place and stronger than ever be observed so
Easily.*

*With his mighty heart, his chivalrous attack,
In the thick of the battle which frightens lions
Of the desert. With the tongue he
Conversed, in his prediction of the future so
Doubtless, as he was always ready, did not
Require any more wonder and thinking.*

*His righteous approaches had no qualm, his
Foresight, and with his determined vision, as
His decisions surpassed Alexander the
Great.*

*With his generous heart he is ready to
Forgive. That convinces traitors to confess,
To regret their sins.*

*To be assured, there is no need to read
Praises of other kings. Look at the stomach
Of poor, are not hungry, as kings firm orders
Would provide grace so plenty.*

When King Saifaldin Adil took over from Saladin's sons, he led campaigns to bring under
his control the lost territories. He sent his
sons to rule them, and he often visited them.
He spent the summer in Syria and winter in
Egypt, as Syria was cool in summer and
Egypt was warm in winter.

The King enjoyed food, sex and a good life.
It was well known that he could eat a grilled
lamb by himself. He was born in Damascus
in June 1145, and died on 31st August 1218,
in a village called Amalikin, near Damascus,
and his body transferred to the Damascus
Castle and later buried in the college's park
that was named after him.

The day of his death coincided with the coming of crusaders invasion of Syria. On his
way of going to face the enemy he died, but
the Crusaders left the battle and headed to
Egypt. He was replaced by his elder son
King Kamil. After two months, Kamil defeated
the crusaders in the battle of *Dumyat* in
North Egypt.

Ibn Khalikan, volume 1 page 489 – 492

Saladin Erbilli 1176 – 1234

Saladin Ahmed, son of Jabir Erbilli, known with the surname of Erbilli, was from a well known family of Erbil, equal to Muzafardin's governor of Erbil. Because of an argument with the governor of Erbil he was imprisoned for a few years, and was released in 1206. He left Erbil and travelled to Syria, accompanied by Emir Qahir Behadin Ayiubid, son of the King Saifadin Adil. He was employed with Emir Muazi al Din, another son of King Saifaldin. After Muazildin died, he left for Egypt and found employment with King Kamil, son of Kig Saifadin Adil, the King of the Ayiubid Empire in Egypt..
He was a well known scientist, essayist, and he knew the works of Abu Hamid Ghazali, in the science of jurisprudence by the name of 'khulasa,' the concise of jurisprudence. He was a poet and a prose writer.

In 1221 when King Kamil with his army were heading to face the crusaders who came to occupy the Mansura region in Egypt, Erbilli's relation with the king was not good. He was arrested and imprisoned in Cairo Castle and was put into solitary confinement. During his imprisonment he started writing essays and poems; and he wrote a lyric for a song, which, when a singer sung the lyrics for King Kamil, the king liked the lyrics and asked who wrote that song. When the king was told that it was written by Saladin Erbilli, he gave order to release him from prison.

Your Order:
Your repressive order to punish someone
Who loves you so much, is it possible to be
Unknown? Your order that made my life to
Be with pain as the days pass.
Your unfair anger is unjustified, as with your
Resentment turned my life so unbearable.
That shows your willingness to terminate my
Life and die.
Whatever you do, seems to be your method,
May need to be done. Is it your desire and
Art? I have not committed any crime but you
Say, yes I had
But, what is there may prevent us to pass a
Night together once more, with having a
Good time with nice discourse.
Until we would set free the rusty anxiety of
Our past, you may forgive me, then I will be
On my way to my love and soon will be back.

When Saladin Erbilli was set free from prison, he returned to his previous high position to work. When Saladin Erbilli was unwell, he seemed to have been frightened of death when he wrote the following:

When You See

When you see your children coming to you
When one is unwell. You should remember
Their coming to you is a prelude to one's
Departure. When they arrived in their Fath-
er's place, then their father should get Ready
for his final journey.

About the day of judgement, he says:

The Day of Judgement

The Day of Judgement is a scary day, as we
Are told about the day; we have to be ready
To do so much goodness to avoid Punish-
ment. That is why in the excursion of Life
there are so many problems, and we Often
end up with so much heartache.

Ibn Unain, a poet from Kuffa, a friend of
Saladin Erbilli, when he was ill, he wrote the
following in a letter to Saladin Erbilli, he says:

*I am declaring to you how I am inflicted and
Face unluckiness from the fortune of life.
When I am a patient, but I have a willingness
To fly to you like a bird, but my wings
Snapped.
I am oppressed and desperate how to find a
Treatment, when I am deprived off seeing
The appearance and well-being of Saladin
Erbilli*

Saladin Erbilli, was born in Erbil in October 1176. Erbilli often socialised with the high ranking officials, as he died when he was with King Kamil in a journey in Anatolia and he fell ill and died in the town of Swaida. His body was taken to the town of Urfa, 'Edissa' in North Kurdistan, in September 1234 and in 1240 one of his sons took his body to Cairo, and reburied in the cemetery of Bokra. He was 60 years old.

Note: Swaida situated in an area called the water source of Orontes

Ibn Khlikan, Volume 1 page, 167 -169

Emir Mukhtar Musbihi 977 – 1045

Emir Mukhtar Musbihi, the son of Qasim son of Ahmed Ismael Abdul Aziz, known as scholar Musbihi. His father came from Haran in North Kurdistan, but he was born in Egypt. He was known as the writer and author of the Egyption history, and was regarded as an authority on the subject. He was known for dressing in military attire at all times. He was a friend of Ubaid son of Aziz, the leader of Egypt.

As it is mentioned in his book, he started working for the leader of Egypt in 1007, after which he became the governor of the town of Port-Saied, in Northern Egypt. He is known to have become the head of *'the Divan Tartib'*

He wrote twelve books about various topics, including: drinking & happiness, meat and sauce, swimming and drowning, fulfilling wishes, stories of the messengers, discussion in creativity, office administration of the future Kings, accounts of the stars, astronomy, coping with depression, questions

and answers, writing lyrics for songs, and a collection of his poetry.
The following example is about a slave girl's death.

To the Slave Girl

Oh, let me take the road that would lead me
To reach God!
Ay, my heart is so broken; I live with pain and
Mourning.
I am shedding tears so much.
How can I overcome the pain of loss, when
She is not here anymore?
Why my love is in the hammock of death?
Oh, that is so enormous infliction, the pain of
Mourning.
Wouldn't it have been the loss of my life and
Soul?
If death had fulfilled my wish of Together-
ness?
When one of the known philosophers goes to
Visit him, who was Ubaidulla son of al Jaw,
He greets him with the following poem:
Now you have brought happiness into my
Heart when you are staying with me
It is such a happiness that may make me fly
Away into the sky
Your scientific wealth has brought on the
Pouring rain of grace.
If it was not for you presence, there would
Not have been any rain.

*With your coming to me there is so much
Aroma of happiness.
It is just like the coming morning of daylight
After the night's darkness.*

Ibn Musbihi's guest was a known poet who had a great sense of humour and was a prolific writer. Musbihi died in Cairo, at the age of ninety-three, and he was buried in the back garden of his house.

Musbihi's son wrote a ballad mourning his father's death:

For Father

When I cannot cope with your departure and
All the tears are not enough
I am facing the feeling of being in despair
And mourning.
The misfortune wears out my heart in the
Cage of my ribs
In such a dreadful situation, no way we can
Deal with fate!
You have stuck your finger nails into my
Heart to be stained with blood.
Oh, destiny you made me put on the Cos-
tume of sadness
Since the one who is a treasure is lying in
The hammock of death
I should have saved him from your hands, as
You are content with your ransom.
As from the distress of losing him almost my
Bones would crash
When his body is going to rot and will turn
Into dust.
Ay, you do now see me so desperate,
Without anticipating any happiness
For when I am struggling in a battle but who
Is to blame?

I lost my father; no one would like to be
Orphaned from early age.
I became so mournful when death
Approached him,
As the collapse of his life has affected me so
Much.

1.   Tartib, is the office of paying salaries.

      Ibn Khalikan volume 3 page 87 - 90

Kamal al Din Ibn Mana 1156 – 1241

Mussa, the son of Fadil, son of Muhamed, son of Mana, also known as Kamal al Din Ibn Mana, was a scholar in the Shafiiet sect. He began his studies with his father in 1175, at Nizamyia College, where he studied with a few more known tutors the science of juris-prudence and philosophy in Mosel, with known scholars like Qurtubi and Qazwini. After he finished his studies he became pro-fessor of the Zaynia school in Mosel, *'Zainyia is taken after the name of Zain al Din, the governor of Erbil at the time. The name of the college was later changed to Kamalyia college after the name of Kamal al Din him-self, Ibn Khalikan studied at this college, as he says.'*

Kamal al Din became a well known scientist in various topics like mathematics. He was known to have knowledge in twenty-four top-ics including philosophy of logic, rhetoric's, and Euclid's, astrology, Ptolemy's astronomy, algebra, accounting physics, meta-physics, Aristotle's agronomy, science of midwifery, medical science and music. As Ibn Khalakn

said, 'he used to be a friend of his father, often visited him, but he had no chance to study with him.'
In a poem about his scientific abilities in the following it says,

In the field of Science had such abilities,
What he knew no one else had knowledge
Of, and the extent of what he knew had no
Equal.
He was such known scholar many came to
Study with him including Jews and Christians
And many other came and flocking to seek
His teaching.
In his praise a North African scholar Emad al
Din Ibn Umar Mkhukh prasised Kamal al Din
In the following poem:
In fact, Kamal al Din has no equal in science
And the cherish of what he produced to such
Extent
In desperation many tries to reach his level
And compete
Whenever the scientist get together to Ana-
lyse, their only reason is to listen to his
Teaching
One should not think that the ones who wear
The turban and insignia of scholarship
Can equal his high level of scholarship, they
Wear those to cover their faces as they Con-
cede.

Once more the same poet says, in the following poem:

When he wore the outfit of his knowledge,
When compared
To other cities are all derelict and empty in
Comparison.
Mosel should understand that the Tigris river
Is proud,
As they both can quench their thirst, and
Their scientific needs.
They are so helpless and their cleverness so
Weak.
One of the like the ocean of waves and
Crystal fresh water,
The other is also an ocean is unequal and so
Unique.
For his high calibre of scientific abilities, the
People branded him worldly and less
Religious.
For the same reason the poet says again:
Seriously I am telling you, the deer is that
Handsome a man I like him so much
The one who never frowned at my
Appearance, and he lets me see him and he
Is my friend
I have my wine mixed with the honey of his
Lips,
So light like the son of Younis, his religious*
Doctrines.

The wine so refreshing, like lines of poetry.

Kamal al Din was born in Mosel, on 30th March 1156, and died on 17th February 1242. He was buried at the Mani's family cemetery that is stated near the Iraq Gate in Mosel.

*Yunus (*Jonah*) was the son of Mitta according to a Tradition quoted in '*Sahih Bukhari*' but the Torah states that his father's name was Amittai. When the prophet hood was conferred upon him, he was commanded to go Nineveh for preaching the true faith of God. Nineveh the ancient name of Mosel, and Yunus is the name of his father, here it has double meaning in the poem.

Ibn Khalikan vol 3 page 466 – 474.

Almanazi the Kurdish Poet, 997 – 1046

Nasr, was the son of Yousif Manazi, a poet and a minster of the governor of Mayfriqan. Ahmed Marwan al Kurdi, was the governor of Mayafriqan, in the Amed region in North Kudistan, South East Turkey. He was a shrewd administrator and was often sent to Constantinople on governmental and diplomatic errands. He busied himself with reading and researching and collecting books. He created a library for the town that was owned by the local authority of the area. The library was open to the local people and scientific research, and the books of this library were known as the Manazie's books. He was a poet himself, and often wrote poems. An example of his poetry when he was travelling through the Valley of Buza, he was inspired by the fresh air and the beauty of the area, he wrote the following:

The Valley of Buza

*The valley that gave us shelter from the
Desert's hot sand*

*Its green thickets created its resting place
Two fold.*

We lie down with the rustling sound of

Its brunches and leaves by the gentle breeze

*Just like mother that stopped feeding her
Toddler*

*And entertained her with sweet melodious
Songs*

That would soon make her happy infant.

*When the summer heat would scorch human
Flesh and so thirsty*

*As we had plenty of fresh water from the
Water spring*

*The water was so sweet, sweeter than the
Generous offer of close friends.*

*In this valley, the walls barred the
Appearance of the sun, as one glanced*

All were shaded. However this did not put a
Barrier to the coming breeze.

The colourful gravels would beautify the
Necklace of the young high ranking lady

With her movements shivered jewels would
Make her nervous if it happened to snap,

And scattered all its beads, and she would
be Sad.

As Ibn Khalikan said, 'this type of poetry was unique and known to belong to him, he published a volume of poetry titled, 'zinat al Dahre'. The judge of Sultan Saladin, Qdi al Fadil tried hard to collect his poems, but was not successful."

- Buza was a small town between Alleppo and Manbij Ibn Khalikan, vol 3 page 126 -128

Almuaid Usulli 1100 – 1162

Saeid Muhamed Usuli, was one of the best poet of the time, he wrote numerous romantic, praises and satirical poems about the leaders in Iraq and Syria. He left a book of poetry behind after he died. He had many friends from poets scholars and scientists, amongst them was Muhib al Din Najar, (*mentioned in vol 1 page 11 of Ibn Khalikans book*) another known poet and a writer on Baghdad history Attafa son of Muhamed, the son of Ali, mentioned this poet as he was born in Alhaditha, and Dujail area near Baquba. He goes to Baghdad at the time of the Abbasid Khalifa Al Mustrarshid Billa to work and study. Usuli wrote many satirical poems about the Abbasid Khlifa Muktafi of Baghdad, he was arrested and sentenced to ten years imprisonment.

Emad al Din Asfahani, Sultan Salaldin's essayist and minster mentioned him in his book, *'Al Kharida,'* as a well-known and ca-pable writer of his time. As he was obtaining fame and wealth, he was imprisoned for writing satirical poems. He spent many years in prison until the Khalifa of Baghdad died, and was replaced by another Khalifa in 1160. As Ibn Khalikan himself met him after he was let free from a dark prison, when he could not see the daylight for years, his eyesight was affected. He also said, 'this poet has always worn army uniform, and after he was freed, he went to Mosel and lived there.' His style of poetry was known to be unique, elegant and tender, especially his romantic poems, and he wrote poems about various topics, for example, he wrote the following poem about pencil:

Pencil

A piece of stick so smooth and straight,

*It is always ready to cause someone's Mis-
ery or to make up someone's wealth.*

*When it promises to provide plenty or signs
The final decision of a conflict.*

*Even before pulling out the sword from its
Sheath,*

*With a written command decides an army's
Defeat.*

*This pencil has been brought from the green
Shoots, the thickets*

*That have been watered to give plenty of
Produce.*

*That was how small streams of water bring
About numerous connections,*

*When announces calamitous pacts of the
Battle-hardened heroes and villains.*

The following poem is about the flute:

The Flute

*This flute's form so beautiful, just like the
Smooth clear melodies of Bulbul*

*With its high pitch, the sound of birds covey
A kind of learning*

*Its quivering harmony, just like dancing of
Branches and leaves.*

*What has it learnt from its infancy from the
Nature's natural happenings?*

*When it gets aged like a scholar's wealth of
Knowledge so plenty for teaching.*

*At the time, it was normal to create Connec-
tions between nature and poetic*

*Visions, as in the following poem again, he
Says:*

The Maid's flute

The young maid is coming with a flute;

It's sound emulated her groovy looks, and
The melody is so fitting

Have a look how these scenes happen to the
Tree! At the time when many birds are
Singing,

Or crying on its green branches so
Passionately.

Until when it's dried, so many would sing

The time goes on unfinished; with the never
Ending noise.

The birds, the strings of the musical
Instruments,

Are two different medium, unaware one form
Other's true existence,

However the happiness of life continues.

Another poem about Flute:

The flute will show two types of happiness:

Salute the man who cut it off the tree

With his hands planted, then to grow fresh
And green.

Pigeons perched with happiness, intimate
With cooing noise until they dry.

A musical maid sings with it, and plays
Various songs and melodies.

In the following poem, he praises King Kamil, son of King Saifuldin Adil, brother of Sultan Saladin:

When he says:

For King Kamil

*The timbers of the mosque's podium are so
Happy,*

*As the king's name is mentioned, they
Remember the time of happiness.*

*When used to be, the fresh green shoot of
The living being.*

Usuli left Baghdad, and died in Mosel in 1064.

His name comes from Usuli or Alusi is the name of a village on the Euphraitis river near Anna & Haditha.

Ibn Khalikan vol 3 page 503 – 508.

Afterword:
These were a few examples of the Kurdish scholars, poets in the history of Islam during the era of the Ayiubid Empire. There were many more scholars and scientists, but I have chosen the poets. Ibn Khaldun, 1332 – 1406, was a founding father of Sociology, a Barber Scholar and philosopher from North Africa. 'Arabs were only interested in being in power and launching expeditions to conquer and occupy others' lands, they were not interested in science, philosophy, that was why many of the scholars were Kurds, Persians, Armenians, even Turks were not known philosophers or scholars in the history of Islam, or even during the Ottoman era, apart from Pharabi.'